CLASSROOM TO CAREER

MY JOB IN
TECHNOLOGY

BY
JOANNA BRUNDLE

PowerKiDS press

New York

Published in 2022 by The Rosen
Publishing Group, Inc.
29 East 21st Street, New York, NY 10010

© 2022 Booklife Publishing
This edition is published by arrangement
with Booklife Publishing

Edited by:
John Wood

Designed by:
Drue Rintoul

Cataloging-in-Publication Data

Names: Brundle, Joanna.
Title: My job in technology / Joanna Brundle.
Description: New York : PowerKids Press,
2022. I Series: Classroom to career I Includes
glossary and index.
Identifiers: ISBN 9781725336506 (pbk.) I
ISBN 9781725336520 (library bound) I ISBN
9781725336513 (6 pack) I ISBN 9781725336537
(ebook)
Subjects: LCSH: Technology--Vocational
guidance--Juvenile literature. I Computer
science--Vocational guidance--Juvenile
literature.
Classification: LCC TA157.5 B767 2022 I
DDC 602.3--dc23

Manufactured in the United
States of America

CPSIA Compliance Information: Batch #CWPK22.
For Further Information contact Rosen Publishing,
New York, New York at 1-800-237-9932.

Find us on 🅕 🅸

CONTENTS

WORDS THAT LOOK LIKE THIS CAN BE FOUND IN THE GLOSSARY ON PAGE 31.

CLASSROOM TO CAREER

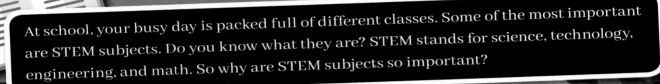

At school, your busy day is packed full of different classes. Some of the most important are STEM subjects. Do you know what they are? STEM stands for science, technology, engineering, and math. So why are STEM subjects so important?

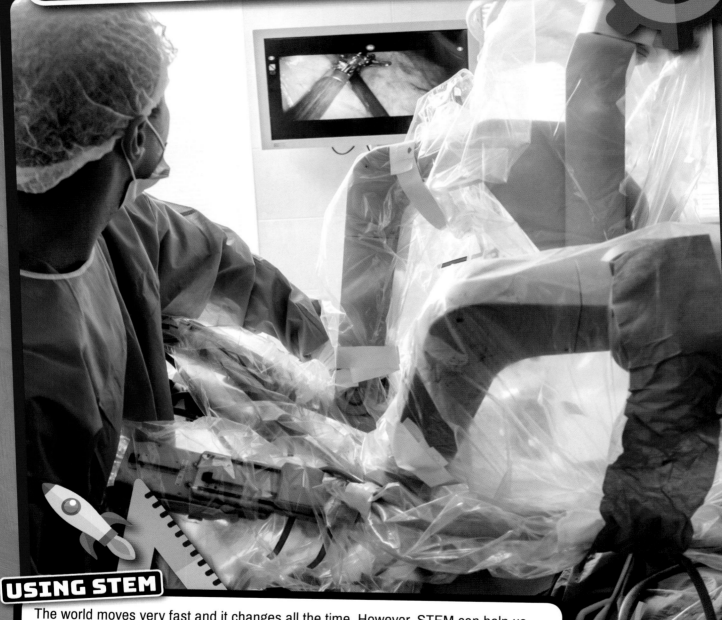

USING STEM

The world moves very fast and it changes all the time. However, STEM can help us understand it. STEM subjects can inspire you to learn more things about how the world works, and they might lead to you working in STEM. Lots of new STEM jobs are being created all the time and in lots of different areas. Who knows what you could be doing in the future? As well as helping you to find interesting work, studying STEM subjects will also help you to solve problems, make decisions, and work as part of a team.

JOB OR CAREER?

A job is something that you do to earn money. Many people stay in jobs for a short amount of time, and they don't always need training. A career is a lifelong work journey in an area that really interests you. People often need the right training for the right career.

Being a vet is a lifelong career.

STEM subjects can help you get into an exciting career, whether you want to be a pilot, a website programmer, or someone who studies dinosaur bones. But STEM subjects are important whatever you do. For example, many careers need you to have computer skills. In this book, we are going to look at technology and the careers it might lead you to.

People who study dinosaur bones are called paleontologists.

WHAT IS TECHNOLOGY?

Technology is the making and using of everyday tools and machines. It includes things such as computing, the internet, and video games. Technology affects every part of our lives, from how you learn in schools to the food you eat.

COMPUTER PROGRAMMER

Are you good with computers? Do you enjoy <u>coding</u>? If so, you have already taken your first steps toward becoming a computer programmer.

Computer programmers create <u>software</u> by writing computer code. Writing computer code involves turning ideas into step-by-step instructions that computers can follow. The work of a computer programmer is difficult, and you will need to be able to work for long periods of time without losing your concentration. Attention to detail is really important because the tiniest coding mistakes can stop a computer program from running correctly.

You might write programs using lots of different computer languages, which are special languages that computers will be able to understand. You will run and test programs to make sure that they work properly and, if not, check the code for mistakes. This is called debugging.

Some computer programmers are trained in one type of computer programming, while others write code for many types of software. You might work for the government, a video game company, or with schools and hospitals. <u>Web-based companies</u> also employ computer programmers to help create web pages.

This programmer is testing a new video game.

Computer programmers may work in a team of computer specialists on a large project, but also work on projects alone. They are usually office-based, but often use email and telephones to work with people from all over the world.

In order to be a computer programmer, you will need a <u>degree</u> in computer science or information systems. You must also know programming languages, for example Java, which is commonly used to build all sorts of things, such as <u>apps</u>.

FORENSIC COMPUTER ANALYST

As technology moves forward, criminals find more and more ways to use it to do something illegal. If you would like to fight crime online, a career as a forensic computer analyst could be for you. The work is interesting, and every digital investigation is different.

Forensic computer analysts use specialist skills of finding and studying data (information), which they use to investigate crimes. These crimes can include hacking, online scams, and data breaches. A data breach is a leak of secret information, such as bank account or credit card details, passwords, and email addresses. Criminals can sell these or use them to buy things illegally. The work of forensic computer analysts involves getting digital evidence, perhaps by taking tablets and mobile phones from a crime scene, then finding and examining data and using it to help catch the criminals. They have to write detailed reports of their findings and may be asked to go to court to show their evidence to others.

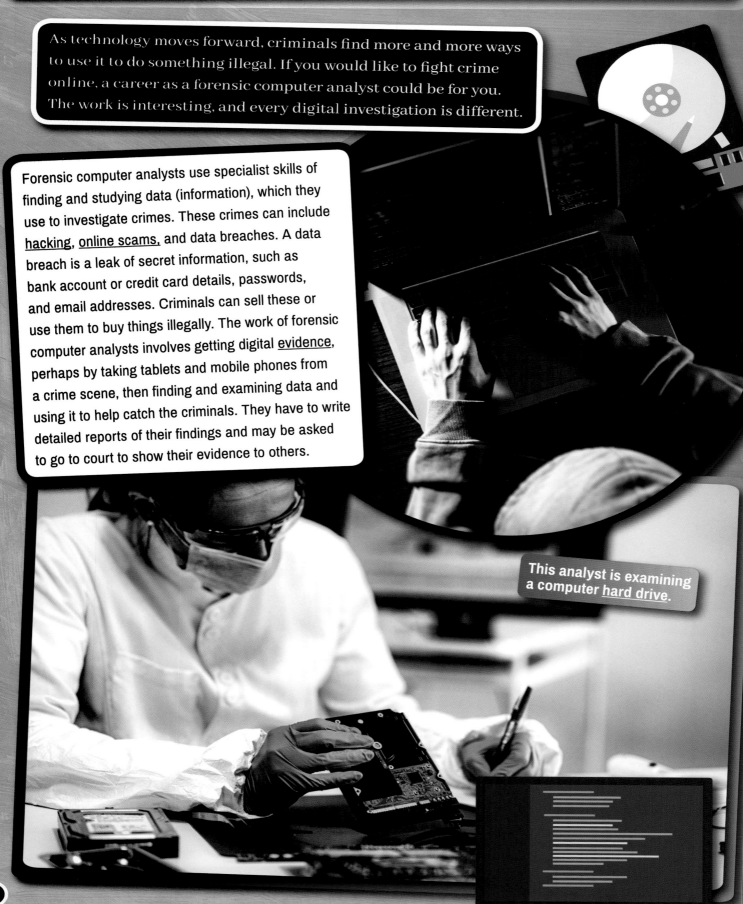

This analyst is examining a computer hard drive.

In the same way that you leave a footprint when you walk, you leave behind a trail of electronic data when you use the internet. This data can be linked directly to you and shows exactly what you have been doing online. It includes emails you send, the websites you have visited, and any information that you have given to online services. Forensic computer analysts follow electronic data trails to discover information about groups of criminals and the links between them.

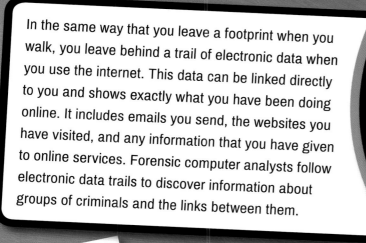

Forensic computer analysts use mobile phones and <u>satellite navigation systems</u> to trace people and link them to crime scenes.

You will need a degree in computer forensics or a similar subject, such as computer science. Forensic computer analysts are employed by the police, by specialist forensics companies, and by large <u>organizations</u> that might face data breaches, such as banks.

FOOD TECHNOLOGIST

Are you a food fanatic? Do you enjoy cooking and inventing weird and wonderful recipes for your family to try? Food technology sounds like the career for you.

Food technologists develop new recipes and change and improve existing ones. They also design the machinery needed to make sure that the food can be made safely and quickly, and that each batch is the same quality. The work also involves making and testing samples before a large amount of the food is created.

These food technologists are testing samples in an ice cream factory.

There are strict laws about how our food is made. Food technologists must make sure that they follow the rules. One of the most important things is that products are correctly labeled. Labels must show the ingredients (what is in the product), allergy advice, <u>nutrition</u> information, "use by" or "best before" date, and storage and cooking instructions. Food technologists carry out experiments to make sure this information is right.

Nutrition Facts

Serving Size 2 Rounded Scoops (4
Serving per Container 20

Amount Per Serving

Calories 150   Calories from Fat 40

	% Daily Value*
Total Fat 3.5g	5%
Saturated Fat 0g	0%
Trans Fat 0g	
Cholesterol 0mg	0%
Sodium 180mg	8%
	2%

Customers' tastes and needs change a lot, so a career in food is always changing too. As a food technologist, you will need to keep coming up with new recipe ideas for customers. Customers may, for example, be looking for fat-free, low-salt foods, or foods with no <u>additives</u>. Plant-based foods are becoming very popular as more people choose a vegetarian or <u>vegan</u> lifestyle.

These vegan burgers are made with chickpeas.

You might also be involved in helping to design food packaging. Food technologists aim to avoid plastic pollution and food waste by developing recyclable packaging that keeps food fresh for longer.

If you would like to be a food technologist, you will usually need a degree in food technology or a similar subject, such as nutrition. Some companies offer internships for students. In an internship, you gain experience by working. In this field, you might be employed by a supermarket chain, a food manufacturing company, or the government.

Work experience in an internship or summer job will help you to find work later.

WEB DEVELOPER

Most organizations and businesses have a website. The job of web developers is to make these websites eye-catching, quick to load, and easy to use. People must be able to connect to the website using all mobile devices, such as tablets and smartphones. Web developers are responsible for the overall look of a website and for things such as speed and how much <u>traffic</u> it can handle without crashing.

You can specialize as either a front-end or back-end developer. Front-end developers build the parts of the website that others see and interact with. They decide the website's layout and put together pictures, sound, and applications, as in the payment section of an online shopping site.

Back-end developers work on the software and <u>databases</u>, and make sure that the website works as expected. Full-stack developers do both front-end and back-end work. UX developers make sure that other people find using the website to be easy and satisfying.

If you would like to be a web developer, you will start off as a junior developer, eventually getting good enough to become a lead developer. You may work on a particular type of website, such as news, shopping, charity, education, or gaming.

JAVA

CSS3

HTML5

HTTP://

If you are employed by a web development company or decide to work for yourself, you will work on lots of different projects at once. You will work on building new sites and updating existing ones. Some developers are employed directly by just one company and spend their time managing and updating that company's website.

A degree in web development or computer science is helpful, but you do not have to have a degree to work as a web developer. You will need to be able to code using different programming languages, and must be able to work both on your own and as part of a team.

ARCHITECTURAL TECHNOLOGIST

Are you creative? Do you like the idea of helping create the buildings of the future? If so, a career as an architectural technologist could be right for you. An architect is someone who designs buildings. In this career, you will use technology to turn designs into working, usable buildings.

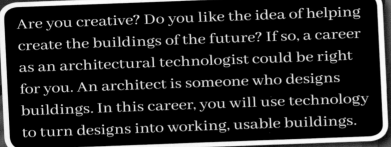

You will meet with customers to talk about projects and find possible places to build. Using CAD (computer-aided design) programs and drawings, you will create designs to show to the customer. Your designs must allow everyone to be able to use a building, including people who use wheelchairs.

Architectural technologists advise clients on any legal and environmental issues and also help to get permission to build there, if it is needed. They advise other people about the materials to build with and the technology and tools needed for the project. As well as dealing with new projects, architectural technologists also give advice on how to repair, improve, or destroy buildings that already exist.

Most of your working day will be spent in an office, but you will also have to carry out site visits. This is to check completed work and to make sure that the project is running smoothly and on time. You might be outdoors in all weather and will have to wear safety equipment on site.

If you would like to be an architectural technologist, you will need a degree in architectural technology or a similar subject, such as civil engineering. Try to find a course that offers you opportunities for work experience in a design office. It will help you understand how projects are handled from start to finish. This is a career that calls for a mixture of technical knowledge and art and design skills.

Safety equipment includes bright vests and hard hats.

Architectural technologists are employed by many different organizations, such as architecture and design offices, building companies, and local government. You may be able to work overseas if you find work with an architectural practice that has offices abroad. Some government departments also have chances to work abroad.

AI DEVELOPER

Human beings are intelligent. This means we have the ability to learn and to solve problems. Artificial intelligence (AI) is the technology that allows a computer to think and learn, copying human intelligence. As this technology moves forward, AI is becoming more and more a part of our lives.

Our <u>social media accounts</u> and smartphones, for example, use AI to discover what we like to do and buy. Streaming services use AI to learn what we watch and listen to, and then suggest other programs or music we might like.

Voice assistants use technology created by AI developers.

Computers need algorithms to learn and solve problems. Algorithms are sets of instructions that a computer can follow, which tell it what to do next and how to work through a problem. Researchers are now exploring technology that allows robots and machines to see and hear like we do.

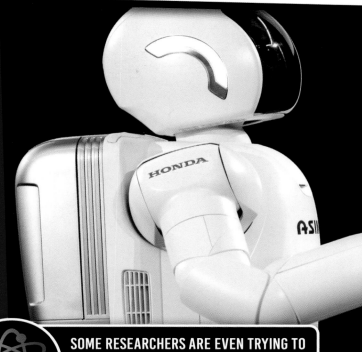

SOME RESEARCHERS ARE EVEN TRYING TO USE AI TO GIVE ROBOTS HUMAN FEELINGS, LIKE HAPPINESS OR EXCITEMENT.

This is ASIMO, a robot that can see and hear. This lets ASIMO interact with humans.

AI developers help to create the software that can be used for artificial intelligence programs and for robots. This software is used in many different ways. In video games, for example, AI is used to make characters that are not controlled by the player, such as enemies and opponents, act in exciting and believable ways. AI is also used in facial recognition software, which can be used to find missing people, track criminals, and unlock smartphones. In hospitals, AI can be used to find out what is wrong with a patient or to program robots used in surgery. As more and more uses are found for AI, the role of the AI developer will be more and more important.

Self Driving

AI is used in driverless vehicles.

If you would like to be part of this fast-moving career, you will need a degree in AI, computer science, or robotics. You will also need mathematical skills and knowledge of computer programming languages.

COMPUTER SUPPORT SPECIALIST

Do you have a talent for solving computer problems? Are you the person in your family that everyone turns to if there is a problem with a computer or internet connection? Maybe you could be a computer support specialist in the future.

Some computer support specialists give technical advice to people. They listen to customers' computer problems, asking questions to find out what is wrong. They then talk customers through the steps they need to take to fix the problem. Other computer support specialists work for an organization where they test computer <u>networks</u> and fix any problems they find. It is important that they back up files to keep all the information safe. Computer support specialists might work in call centers, helping customers or businesses with IT problems.

This computer support specialist is working in a call center.

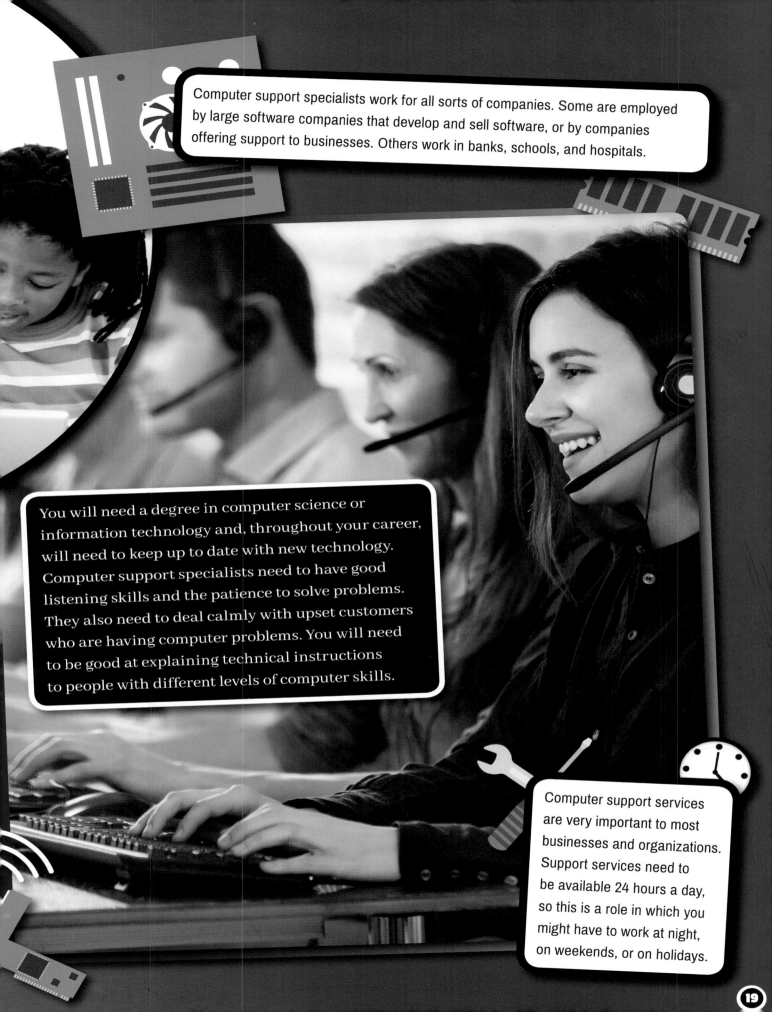

Computer support specialists work for all sorts of companies. Some are employed by large software companies that develop and sell software, or by companies offering support to businesses. Others work in banks, schools, and hospitals.

You will need a degree in computer science or information technology and, throughout your career, will need to keep up to date with new technology. Computer support specialists need to have good listening skills and the patience to solve problems. They also need to deal calmly with upset customers who are having computer problems. You will need to be good at explaining technical instructions to people with different levels of computer skills.

Computer support services are very important to most businesses and organizations. Support services need to be available 24 hours a day, so this is a role in which you might have to work at night, on weekends, or on holidays.

BIOTECHNOLOGIST

Biotechnologists study <u>cells</u> and the living tissue that makes up our bodies. They study this in order to develop new technology that will improve our lives. Biotechnology is a fast-growing career.

Medical biotechnologists develop treatments and cures. They also create vaccines, which are injected into people to protect them from diseases. Agricultural biotechnologists <u>genetically modify</u> crops. This means more crops can be grown, and fewer will be destroyed by bugs.

Environmental biotechnologists research renewable sources of energy, such as using plants to create <u>biofuels</u>. They also find new ways to deal with pollution and waste and create <u>biodegradable materials</u>, including plastics made from plants. Industrial technologists make <u>enzymes</u> that improve the flavor of food and drinks and keep them fresh for longer.

As a biotechnologist, you might collect and test samples of cells, tissues, blood, and bacteria and then carry out experiments. You will then study your results to see what you have discovered.

Stain removers and energy-saving detergents that work in cold water have been created by biotechnologists.

BIOFUEL

BIONIC TECHNOLOGY

Bionic technology is an exciting part of modern medicine. Bionics is the creation of human-made things, such as replacement limbs, that are similar to living things. Replacement limbs have been around for centuries, but bionic limbs now include a 3D-printed arm, with a hand that can be used to pinch, fist bump, and high-five like a real hand. In the future, there may be computer chips that could replace parts of the brain that have been damaged by diseases.

Biotechnologists are employed by a wide range of employers. These include hospitals, <u>pharmaceutical companies</u>, and companies involved with food, crops, and the environment.

3D PRINTING IS THE PROCESS OF MAKING AN OBJECT FROM A COMPUTER DESIGN.

Laboratory

If you want to be a biotechnologist, you'll need a degree in a science subject, such as biotechnology or environmental biology. Try to find a course that includes work opportunities. Work experience allows you to work in a laboratory and improve your skills.

IT TRAINER

If you love using computers and would like to help other people to use them too, a career as an IT trainer could be right for you.

IT trainers plan and carry out training courses covering lots of computer skills. They might teach skills involving commonly used programs, such as spreadsheets, or more technical skills, such as programming. You may deliver training on particular programs used by the company that employs you, such as a new system for billing customers.

Your work as an IT trainer will involve working out the type of training that is needed and then creating the right training course. You will need to design all the course materials, such as training booklets and handouts. You will also be responsible for setting up the training room, including any IT equipment that is needed. For online learners, you will need to design e-learning resources. After giving your training sessions, you will decide whether more training is needed.

You will sometimes work in a classroom. Sometimes you may work as a floor walker. This involves walking around an office, dealing with workers' questions or problems.

You might use floor walking after a training session to give learners confidence in using their new skills to carry out their work.

Ideally, you will need a degree in computing or business management. You will need some knowledge of teaching. You must be good at talking to people and you must be patient, as you will have learners from all backgrounds. You might be employed by a training provider, a university, or any organizations that use IT, such as hospitals. Once you have enough experience, you could set up your own training company.

ASSISTIVE TECHNOLOGY TRAINING

Assistive technology is any technology that helps people with disabilities to carry out tasks. If you like the idea of teaching people with disabilities to use computers, you could specialize as an assistive technology trainer, helping people to use technology such as speech input software. This helps a person to type text and control a computer using their voice.

Professor Stephen Hawking used assistive technology that allowed him to write books and give speeches.

MULTIMEDIA ARTIST OR ANIMATOR

Multimedia artists and animators create 2D and 3D models, animations (images that appear to move), and visual effects for TV programs, films, video games, and music videos. They do this by using drawings and computer programs. If you love art and design, but also have strong computer skills, you should consider this career choice.

After the design stage, film directors, game designers, and other artists will ask you to make changes to improve your work. You will need to work closely with other members of your team, as you will all be working on different parts of a project that must be brought together to create a finished animation.

Multimedia artists or animators often specialize in a particular area, such as video games or animated films. You may use technology known as CGI — computer-generated imagery. CGI is the use of computers to create 3D special effects and images, in both animated films and those with live actors.

You might choose to specialize even further. As a video game artist, for example, you might specialize in level design, in which you would be responsible for the layout, look, and feel of different levels of the game. In animated movies, you might specialize in the backgrounds or in animating main characters.

You might choose to work using computer software or to write your own computer code. Some artists, however, begin by drawing and painting by hand before putting these designs into computer programs. If you work for an animation company, you will usually find that they have their own animation software, which you will have to learn to use.

In order to work in this field, you will need a degree in computer graphics, art, or animation. You must also have both creative, artistic talents and computer skills. Many multimedia artists or animators are self-employed, while others work for film, video, and TV companies or computer systems designers.

A storyboard is a sequence of sketches that maps out the different scenes for a video game or film.

CYBERSECURITY SPECIALIST

Are you great at using computers? Do you enjoy solving difficult puzzles? Do you keep going when everyone else has given up? If so, you could consider a career as a cybersecurity specialist.

Cybercrime is the word used for crimes that are carried out using computers or the internet. Computer hackers and organized gangs of cybercriminals are constantly coming up with new ways to carry out cybercrime. The role of the cybersecurity specialist is to stay one step ahead. Any computer that is connected to the internet could be a target for cybercrime and it is becoming more and more common. This means cybersecurity specialists are needed.

There are many types of cybercrime, including stealing secret information, spreading computer viruses, and carrying out phishing scams to get people's bank details.

Your work will involve designing new security systems and updating existing ones. You will need to research new cybersecurity threats and find ways to deal with them. You will look for weaknesses in an organization's system and find the best way of keeping it safe by using things such as firewalls.

You will need to always be on the lookout for any signs of a cyberattack, be ready to act quickly to find out how an attack may have happened, and be prepared to stop it as quickly as possible. You may also carry out "ethical hacking." This means carrying out a simulated (pretend) attack, to find any weaknesses in an organization's systems or to check how well existing cybersecurity systems are working.

1001
0110

Cybersecurity specialists work for universities, banks, airlines, the armed forces, and the government. In fact, any large company or organization with a database is likely to need the help of a cybersecurity specialist.

You will need a degree in a STEM subject or in computer science. Knowledge of computer hardware, software, and networks is important. You must be patient and look at every little detail to solve complicated problems. At times, you will have to think like a cybercriminal to work out what they have done or might try next.

Part of your work might be to give cybersecurity training to your colleagues.

DATABASE ADMINISTRATOR

Are you great with computers? Are you a super-organized person? If so, a career as a database administrator could be right for you.

A database is a set of data stored electronically in a computer system. As a database administrator, you will use specialist software to organize and store data, so that the right information is available to the right people when they need it. You will also be responsible for testing the database and keeping it up to date.

You will help to protect the security of the data by controlling who is allowed to log in and see the database. You will check who has used the database and why they needed to. Database administrators are also responsible for checking that data is backed up and for coming up with disaster recovery plans, so an organization can keep working if the data is lost in an emergency.

You will need to make sure that the database has enough space to add more data if needed.

NODE 01

NODE 04

NODE 05

NODE 03

BLOCK 01

NODE 02

```
operation == "MIRROR_X":
mirror_mod.use_x = True
mirror_mod.use_y = False
mirror_mod.use_z = False
operation == "MIRROR_Y"
mirror_mod.use_x = False
mirror_mod.use_y = True
mirror_mod.use_z = False
operation == "MIRROR_Z":
mirror_mod.use_x = False
mirror_mod.use_y = False
mirror_mod.use_z = True

selection at the end -add
ob.select= 1
er_ob.select=1
context.scene.objects.activ
"Selected" + str(modifier
irror_ob.select = 0
bpy.context.selected_ob
data.objects[one.name].se

int("please select exactl

  OPERATOR CLASSES ----

types.Operator):
  X mirror to th
ject.mirror_m
ror X"

context):
ext
```

The Data Protection Act is an important law that protects people's personal information and how it is used. Part of your job will be to make sure that your employer is following the law.

Database administrators are needed by any organization that stores large amounts of data. Governments, IT companies, banks, credit card companies, hospitals, and universities are examples of organizations that might employ you.

You will ideally need a degree in a computer-based subject, but there are also opportunities for people who leave school and then train "on the job." You must have great computer skills, especially in database technology, covering design and software.

TECHNOLOGISTS WHO HAVE CHANGED THE WORLD

BILL GATES

Bill Gates is a software designer and businessman who, along with his business partner Paul Allen, developed one of the biggest software companies in the world. Together with his wife Melinda, Bill Gates used the wealth that the company produced to set up a charity. The charity aims to help people out of poverty and to improve education and health care for all.

SUSAN KARE

In the 1980s, graphic designer Susan Kare designed many famous symbols and fonts for computers. Some of them, such as the trash can and paintbrush, are still in use today.

Susan Kare designed the cmd symbol, among many others.

GRACE HOPPER

Grace Hopper helped to create the first electronic computer, invented one of the first programming languages, and invented the first compiler, a program that changes code into instructions that can be "understood" by a computer.

MARY JACKSON

Mary Jackson was a mathematician who worked for NASA, the U.S. <u>space agency</u>. She was the first African American engineer to work for NASA. Her work focused on how air flows around aircraft, and this research helped send people to space.

GLOSSARY

additives	substances added to food to preserve or improve its flavor or appearance
apps	short for applications – computer programs designed for a particular purpose and often downloaded by a user to a mobile device
biodegradable materials	substances that can be broken down naturally by the action of microorganisms
biofuels	fuels made from living materials
cells	the basic building blocks that make up all living things
coding	the process of creating software
databases	sets of data held in computers
degree	a qualification in a specialist subject, often given by a university or college to people usually over the age of 18
enzymes	substances produced by living organisms that speed up chemical reactions
evidence	proof
facial recognition software	software that can recognize a person from their unique facial features
firewalls	network security systems that stop illegal access to a computer that is connected to the internet
genetically modify	change the genetic makeup of a living organism
hacking	illegally breaking into a computer network for criminal purposes
hard drive	a computer storage system that is used to store data permanently
hardware	the physical parts of a computer system
networks	sets of computers connected together
nutrition	nourishment ("goodness") or energy obtained from food
online scams	tricks intended to deceive people, carried out on the internet
organizations	groups, companies, or businesses
pharmaceutical companies	businesses that research, develop, and sell medicines
phishing	an online trick that tries to make people give away secret information
satellite navigation systems	computer-operated systems that use satellite signals to pinpoint where a user is and give directions to a destination
social media accounts	websites and apps that people use to connect with others
software	the programs or instructions that tell a computer how to work
space agency	a government organization that researches and explores space
traffic	the flow of data passing through a computer system
vegan	a diet and way of life that does not use or consume products from animals
web-based companies	businesses that customers access using the internet

INDEX

Photo Credits

Images are courtesy of Shutterstock.com. With thanks to Getty Images, Thinkstock Photo and iStockphoto.
2&3 – Dmitry Fokin. 4&5 – Roman Zaiets, Rido, paleontologist natural. 6&7 – Sashkin, Akhenaton Images, G-Stock Studio, LDprod, Oberon. 8&9 – Mike_shots, Microgen, Denys Prykhodov, Photo Spirit, Eny Setiyowati, Iurii Kiliian, D.R.3D, Ellagrin. 10&11 – Syda Productions, Ekaterina_Minaeva, Nina Firsova, Phovoir, Dacian G. 12&13 – ProStockStudio, Rawpixel.com, Amnaj Khetsamtip, Elle Aon, 1ZiMa, Lia Ristiana. 14&15 – Lucky Business, Myroslava Malovana, yoshi0511, Macrovector, Iconic Bestiary. 16&17 – Zapp2Photo, catwalker, HQuality, metamorworks, Anatolir, CloudyStock, Ico Maker. 18&19 – wavebreakmedia, Gorodenkoff, Andrey_Popov, Macrovector, Equipoise. 20&21 – Budimir Jevtic, Ociacia, Maridav, Andrey_Popov, Gorodenkoff, hvostik, A Aleksii, Titov Nikolai, Anna_leni, bakinova_art, Abscent. 22&23 – Phovoir, dotshock, fizkes, Twocoms, vasabii, Sabelskaya. 24&25 – Dream Expander, Gorodenkoff, Chaosamran_Studio, sasha2109, Bloomicon. 26&27 – Gorodenkoff, sdecoret, Rawpixel.com, Anatolir. 28&29 – Gorodenkoff, whiteMocca, Joe Techapanupreeda, Macrovector. 30 – Frederic Legrand – COMEO, daniiD.